A Dish Called Vonda

By Vonda E McIntosh

Menus for Entertaining at Home

First Published in Great Britain
by Vonda McIntosh 1999

Set in Rotis Serif Italic & New Berolina MT by Harley & Cox

Printed and bound by Harley & Cox Ltd., Dundee, Scotland

ISBN 0 9537294 0 0

All recipes used in this book have been adapted for my own use, and the methods kept simple and straight forward.

Front Cover Photographs - Richard Scott Thomson
Digital Design - Max & Co., Aberdeen
E-mail: vonda.mcintosh@btinternet.com

A Dish called Vonda
Menus for Entertaining at Home
By Vonda E McIntosh

Contents:

Acknowledgements

To friends at home and abroad who have shared with me their favourite recipes.

To John Tovey, proprietor of the famous Miller Howe Hotel, Windermere, for his generosity in allowing me to share with you some of his recipes.

To Richard Scott Thomson for his beautiful photographs. He has captured and enhanced my original ideas of showing the raw ingredients rather than the finished dish.

To Frances Montgomery for her patience and dedication typing this book, from the first hand written notes, to the finished copy. We both worked hard to meet our deadlines, her's took nine months,(a beautiful little girl called Beth) mine took a little longer!

Dedication

This book is dedicated to my family (especially the Tervit Clan), my good friends, and 'my ladies' who have all given me encouragement and support when I needed it most.

When I told 'my ladies' I was writing a Cookery Book they all said "good"!

I hope this is good enough!

Introduction

This book was conceived after the fun and satisfaction I found from writing a personalised cookery book as part of a wedding gift for Garith, my cousin's son. He would phone me from University asking for cookery tips and recipes and so I wrote the recipe book as if I was talking to him. I believe the book is now well worn after two years of continual use!

Cooking has been my life, and over the years cooking and demonstrating dishes to the public have been immensely rewarding. For me, showing someone how easy it is for them to cook a meal at home, then afterwards having them tell me it was easy, is the greatest compliment. This book is not to teach people how to cook, just show how easy it is to cook without fuss, and avoid anxiety when entertaining at home.

Entertaining should be a pleasure and if it is not, then perhaps this book can help. (I have been demonstrating this for over 30 years so I must be doing something right!).

Unfortunately entertaining at home is not just about cooking an enjoyable meal for friends or colleagues, it involves much more! Shopping, preparation, setting the table, feeding the children and pets, (where applicable) clearing away kitchen clutter, and not forgetting the inspection of the downstairs loo. All this has to be done before guests arrive and 10 minutes before they arrive you find time to 'dress for dinner'. Sounds familiar? Of course it does, because we've all gone through it!

Over the many years I've been giving classes on "Entertaining at Home", the same concerns are always voiced. Not knowing what recipes to put together as a menu and how to cook these dishes to be ready when the guests are ready!

So I have compiled complete menus for each month of the year, taking in seasonal foods, and using these to create menus, bringing in colours and textures to compliment the feel of the month. (Apologies if it snows in June!).

Our tastes have definitely changed over the years, and apart from the obvious swing to healthier eating, we have lost interest in recipes involving time-consuming preparations and infinite patience to assemble. (That is what I expect when I go out for dinner to a restaurant). What we need are recipes where most of the work is done a few hours before hand, then when our guests arrive we simply do the last minute preparations, cook and serve when we are ready to eat.

Follow my simple rule of A.B.C and all will be well!

A. *Always check beforehand if your guests have any food dislikes or allergies. This could be disastrous if you only find out when the dish is served at the table.*

B. *Ban husbands, partners, children and pets from the kitchen while cooking (no one to blame or annoy you).*

C. *Cook only what you know will work and recipes you have tried and tasted before. (Less stress all around).*

Lastly, drink a glass of wine while you prepare, helps you relax! Don't' skimp on butter and fresh cream when entertaining, you go back on diet tomorrow!

Conversion Tables

	STATIC OVEN SETTING ELECTRICITY		GAS MARK	FAN ASSIST OVEN SETTING
	F	C		
VERY COOL	225	110	1/4	85
	250	130	1/2	105
COOL	275	140	1	110
	300	150	2	120
MODERATE	325	170	3	135
	350	180	4	145
MOD. HOT	375	190	5	150
	400	200	6	160
HOT	425	220	7	175
	450	230	8	185
VERY HOT	475	240	9	200

Measurements

IMPERIAL . . . . .METRIC

1 oz 25g
2 oz 50g
3 oz 75g
4 oz (1/4 lb) . . . . .100 – 125g
5 oz 150g
6 oz 175g
7 oz 200g
8 oz (1/2 lb) 225g
9 oz 250g
10 oz 275g
11 oz 300g
12 oz (3/4 lb) 350g
13 oz 375g
14 oz 400g
15 oz 425g
16 oz (1lb) 450g

AMERICAN . . . . .METRIC

1/8cup 25ml
1/4 cup 50ml
1/3 cup 100ml
1/2 cup 150ml
2/3 cup 175ml
3/4 cup 200ml
1 cup 225ml
1-1 1/2 cup 300ml
2 cups 400ml
2 1/2 cups 500-600ml
3 cups 700ml
3 3/4 cups 900ml
4 1/4 cups . . . . .1 litre
. . . . .1.1 litre
. . . . .1.3 litre
. . . . .1.4 litre

P.S. A little extra help for my North American friends:-

U.K. Measurements
1 pt (20 fl. ozs)	=	17 ozs
1/2 pt (10 fl. ozs)	=	8 1/2 ozs

U.K. Spoons
1 tablespoon	=	1 x 25 ml. spoon or 2 x 15 ml.
1 dessertspoon	=	1 x 15 ml. spoon
1 teaspoon	=	1 x 5 ml. spoon

U.K. Teacup
(using raw long grain rice as an example)

1 heaped teacup	=	1 American 240 ml./8 oz cup
	or	1 Canadian cup

May I suggest you use a U.K. measuring jug and scales to help with recipes,
rather than trying to convert, it does make it easier – honest!

I'm an old fashioned cook, I still use
Imperial Measures for all recipes.
These tables will help you convert weights and measures.

January Menu

Orange and Carrot Soup

Chicken with Brandied Prunes

Baked Potatoes with Cream and Cheese

Broccoli Florets
Carrots with Butter and Parsley

Hot Buchan Raspberry Pudding

Orange and Carrot Soup

This wonderful soup comes from John Tovey. His basic recipe for all cream soup is the same, only adding different ingredients for the change in flavours. You've probably never done this method before but once tasted you'll never go back to any other method.

P.S. You need greaseproof or wax paper!

Ingredients:-

2 lb carrots

2 ozs butter

8 ozs onions (2 medium)

1/4 pt dry sherry

1/2 teaspoon salt

freshly ground black pepper

1 pt stock

1/2 pt fresh orange juice

1 tablespoon castor sugar

Method:-

Using a large saucepan, melt the butter slowly. Peel and chop the onion and add to butter, cook gently and do not allow to brown. Clean carrots and cut into large slices, then add to saucepan. Stir well; add sherry, seasoning and castor sugar (it's finer than granulated so will dissolve quicker without sticking to pan) stir well. This is now where it differs from other soup recipes. Tear off a double thickness of greaseproof paper, run it under the cold water tap to dampen it and squeeze out excess water and flatten it, still double, and place on top of ingredients in saucepan. Place on lid, and allow to simmer over a low heat for 45 minutes or until the carrots are soft. (This method allows all the flavour and natural juices to be retained in the saucepan instead of evaporating). When the carrots are soft, (test with a skewer) remove the paper, add the stock and orange juice, then liquidize the soup and pour into a clean pan. At this stage, taste and adjust seasoning then leave to one side until ready to reheat. (Don't reheat all of soup if you only require 4 – 6 portions). To serve, reheat until a gentle boil, do not bubble boil, pour out into hot soup bowls and garnish with a swirl of double cream (take a dessert spoonful of double cream and drizzle over top of soup) sprinkle with chopped parsley or grated raw carrot.

Useful hints:-

As I never make a small pan of soup, this amount of soup will give you 8 generous portions. Any leftover can be used the following day or can be frozen. Dry sherry is used in the recipe but medium or cream will do - just reduce the amount of sugar you add with the carrots. Use the best of stock, chicken or turkey gives a wonderful flavour, however being realistic, chicken or vegetable stock cubes will work perfectly.

Chicken and Brandied Prunes

This is a favourite of mine as I love the richness and flavour the prunes give to the sauce, and with no additional cream added, it's good for you!

Ingredients:-
(Serves 4)

4 chicken fillets

1/4 pt brandy

20 prunes (approximately 8 oz packet)

1/2 oz unsalted butter (or slightly salted butter)

1 onion

1 carrot

4 cloves garlic

1 teaspoon dry mustard

1 teaspoon fresh or 1/4 teaspoon dried thyme

1 pt chicken stock

parsley stalks (approx. 5 – 6, reserve leaves for garnish)

3 tablespoons lemon juice

Method:-

Pour brandy over prunes and if possible leave to soak overnight. If not, soak for the maximum time available. Melt butter in frying pan and brown fillets quickly on both sides. Transfer to a casserole dish. (If no casserole dish, oven proof dish with lid, or cover with tin foil). Finely chop onion and slice carrot and quickly sauté in frying pan, spoon into casserole. Add prunes, brandy liquid, stock, garlic cloves (peeled but left whole) mustard, thyme, parsley stocks and a little seasoning. (Remember if you're using stock cubes for stock don't add additional salt as cubes are quite salty). At this stage, leave in a cool place until ready for cooking. Place in oven and cook for approximately 1 hour at 170° C.

Before serving we need to reduce the liquid until it's a sauce consistency, so if the casserole dish can go directly onto the heat, first remove parsley stocks and garlic cloves, add lemon juice and reduce for approximately 10 minutes. If using an ovenproof dish, pour the liquid out into a saucepan, quickly reduce and return sauce to chicken. Mix well and serve onto hot plates. Have the parsley ready either in bunches or chopped to sprinkle over chicken.

Useful hints:-

Fillets are all meat.

Breasts can have part of the wing bone attached.

Portions are the breasts still with the rib cage bones underneath.

Thighs and Legs I don't recommend for entertaining.

John Tovey gave me a taste of this recipe and it's absolutely wonderful, great for using up old potatoes, old cheese and not so new or defrosted cream. It bakes in the oven along with any main course.

Select either all the same size potatoes to cook whole, or cut up large ones into even size pieces, allowing 2 - 4 per person.

Ingredients:-

8 – 12 potato pieces

2 – 4 ozs white cheddar cheese (either medium or mature)

1/2 pt whipping or double cream

Method:-

Boil potatoes until par boiled (soft but not cooked). Drain carefully and place in ovenproof dish (lightly buttered) evenly spaced in one layer. Pour over cream and sprinkle with cheddar cheese. (Cream has to come halfway up potatoes, so choose your dish wisely!!) Leave in a cool place until ready to cook. Bake approximately for 1 hour (same as chicken, see!) To serve, sprinkle with chopped parsley.

Broccoli florets

1 lb broccoli

1 oz butter

freshly ground pepper

Cut all florets off stalks and cut into even sized pieces. Peel stalk to expose soft green centre. (This too can be sliced and cooked with florets). At this stage, blanch (see notes below) and leave until ready to cook. Cook in boiling salted water for 5 – 7 minutes. Drain, toss with butter and pepper.

Julienne of Carrots

1 lb carrots (use 1 carrot per person)

1 oz butter

Chopped parsley (about 2 tablespoons)

Prepare carrots and cut into as fine strips as possible (as thin as you dare!). Blanch and leave until ready to cook. Cook in boiling salted water for 5 – 7 minutes. Toss in butter and parsley.

Useful hints:-

If not using previously prepared frozen vegetables, most vegetables can be cleaned, prepared, cut and blanched ready for use in the evening. To blanch vegetables, drop into boiling water, bring back to boil, drain and chill quickly with running cold water. Drain well, place in saucepans or keep in polythene bags until ready to cook for meal.

Hot Buchan Raspberry Pudding

This is a lovely clean tasting dessert and one which uses up raspberries from the freezer. (Buchan means from the Aberdeenshire area).

Ingredients:-
(Serves 4)

1 lb frozen raspberries (slightly defrosted and drained)

3 tablespoons castor sugar

1/2 pt sour cream

2 eggs (medium)

1 tablespoon plain flour

Method:-

Place the raspberries into a shallow ovenproof dish (I use a flan dish), and sprinkle with 2 tablespoons sugar. Beat cream with eggs, add flour and remaining sugar. Mix well and pour over raspberries. Bake at 150°C for approximately 45 minutes until golden brown. Allow to cool a little before serving. Serve with pouring cream or fromage frais.

Useful hints:-

To prepare beforehand, have raspberries in dish. Have cream and eggs in a bowl, all other ingredients ready to hand. Just before you start to serve the meal, follow the method and bake in the oven as directed, or alternatively bake just before your guests arrive and serve cool.

February Menu

Onion and Walnut Quiche

Bon Accord Pork Casserole

Creamy Baked Potatoes

Petit Pois with Shallots

Mange Tout

Crêpes Suzette

Onion and Walnut Quiche

This is an unusual quiche as it uses puff pastry for the flan base instead of shortcrust pastry. Once you've tried this quiche you can use it time and again as a starter or luncheon, and it's great for vegetarian friends. If you don't like walnuts use pecan nuts instead. Always use cream in a quiche!

Ingredients:-
(Serves 8 – 10 as a starter or 4 – 5 for lunch)

12 oz packet frozen puff pastry (defrost for approximately 1 hour)

1 lb onions

1/2 oz butter

1 clove garlic

1/2 teaspoon soft brown sugar (light muscovado)

3 ozs chopped walnuts

4 ozs cream cheese

5 fl oz carton double cream

2 eggs (medium)

seasoning

fresh nutmeg

Before you start give yourself plenty of room to roll out the pastry, and have plain flour to dust the pastry while rolling out. Remember to roll the pastry one way only, turn the pastry not the rolling pin! (You know the reasons, if not, ask me!).

Method :-

Now roll the pastry out, and line a flan dish. The 12 oz packet will allow you to keep the pastry fairly thick, and it should remain a square at all times!!! Make sure you press well into the flutes and bring the pastry up the sides with a little over the top. Trim off the excess with a sharp knife. While you prepare the filling, pop the flan into the refrigerator to keep cool.

Peel onions, cut in half, finely slice and sauté in the melted butter until soft. Add garlic and sugar, then stir and cook a little more. Add chopped walnuts, stir well and spoon over base of pastry. Break up cream cheese with fingers (using a knife is messy) and dot lumps of cheese (about the size of a walnut) over the filling. Beat eggs with cream until well mixed, season with a little salt and freshly ground black pepper and pour over flan. Grate fresh nutmeg over the top. Bake at 190°C for a minimum of 35 minutes. (Do not peek into oven before 30 minutes or the filling will collapse!) Bake until well risen and golden brown. It looks impressive when you bring it out of the oven, so make sure your guests see it! The quiche will give you a maximum of 8 – 10 portions as a starter – its such an easy beginning to a meal. To serve as a starter, have prepared individual garnishes on plates. Perhaps tossed green salad leaves in a walnut oil dressing (prepare first in a bowl) with a curled slice of orange or tomato, or 2 – 3 stalks of blanched asparagus. Looks great!

Useful hints:-

If you want to prepare beforehand, fill pastry flan with onions, walnuts and cheese. Beat eggs with cream and leave separate at this stage in a cool place, then 45 minutes before you want to eat, pour custard over filling and cook as directed.

If you are wondering what "flutes" are, it's the wavy edge of the flan dish!

Bon Accord Pork Casserole

Sometimes a casserole dish is ideal for entertaining if you're off doing things with your guests. This can be prepared, or even cooked and frozen beforehand, so all it needs is re-heating. Casseroles are great too for increasing the quantity to cover extra guests. I've prepared this recipe for 20 people.

Ingredients:-
(Serves 4 – 6)

2 lb pork (shoulder, if you have time to cube and remove excess fat, if not, use fillet).

2 tablespoons plain flour

salt and pepper

2 onions (medium)

6 ozs mushrooms

1 tablespoon oil

1 oz butter

1/2 pt sweet cider

1 chicken stock cube

2 tablespoons tomato puree

Method:-

Cut pork into cubes, mix flour with seasoning and toss pork in it. Heat oil and butter in saucepan and fry the pork quickly until sealed, preferably in small amounts so it seals quickly, otherwise the moisture comes out of pork and you end up with too much liquid in the pan. Transfer to an ovenproof dish or casserole dish. Peel and chop onions, wipe and slice mushrooms and quickly sauté all in saucepan. Spoon out onto pork. Empty remaining flour into saucepan, gradually pour in cider, stock cube and tomato puree and mix until it comes to the boil. Pour over pork, and carefully mix it all together. Cover and cook for approximately 2 hours at 160°C or until pork is tender. Garnish with chopped parsley.

Useful hints:-

As cultivated mushrooms are usually clean, there is no need to wash or peel them. Simply wipe off excess dirt with a kitchen paper towel.

Creamy Baked Potatoes / Petit Pois with Shallots

This is an easy way to use old potatoes and it looks a little more special than simply mashing them.

Ingredients:-

2 lb potatoes

1 egg

1/4 pint milk

1/2 oz butter

Method:-

Cook potatoes and mash. Allow to cool a little, then add the beaten egg, milk, butter and freshly ground pepper. Mix well until soft and creamy. Butter a shallow ovenproof dish, spoon out potatoes and spread evenly, mark with a fork or knife. Dot with extra butter pieces, and leave until ready to cook in the oven at 170°C for 20 – 30 minutes until golden brown. (If cooking with the pork casserole, cook at the lower temperature but increase length of cooking time).

Petit Pois with Shallots - (Serves 4 - 6)

1 lb frozen petit pois (baby peas)

3 shallots (member of the onion family)

1 oz butter

Melt butter in saucepan, peel and chop shallots and sauté until soft. Meanwhile boil peas as instructed on the packet for 3- 5 minutes, drain and empty into butter and shallots. Toss well and serve. (The shallots give interest to the peas – leave out if you prefer plain peas). Serve mange tout or green beans tossed in melted butter if you wish more vegetables.

Crêpe Suzette

As we remember Shrove Tuesday this month, I though this dessert would be appropriate. I enjoy making crêpes, however the secret does lie in using the correct pan. A crêpe pan is not the same as a frying pan, so invest in a good quality pan, large or small, and you will be amazed how easy they are to make. Crêpes can be made in advance on the day, stack them up on a plate (they don't stick together) and cover with a clean tea towel. You can also freeze them, but allow time for defrosting.

Ingredients:-
(Serves 4 – 6)

Batter:-

4 ozs plain flour

1 egg (medium)

1/2 pt milk

Suzette sauce

2 oranges, zest and juice

1 lemon, zest and juice

8 – 10 sugar lumps (at last a use for them)

1/2 oz unsalted butter

2 tablespoons of orange liquer or Drambuie (optional for flambé)

Method:-

Put flour in bowl, drop in egg and with wire whisk, mix in milk slowly until it's a runny batter. Pour into a measuring jug and leave to rest for 10 – 30 minutes if possible. Heat crêpe pan until hot, wipe over with a little oil on a piece of kitchen paper towel and pour a little of the batter into the pan, lifting and moving the pan until the batter covers the bottom. Don't worry if the first few are hit or miss – too much batter – pour it back into the jug, too little, spoon a little batter over the holes! You'll get the hang of it quickly, and as the batter bubbles, using a palette knife, turn it over (or toss if the moods right!) Oil the pan for each crêpe made, and stack them on a plate. This quantity will give you 12 – 15 small crêpes. Now you have the crêpes made, use when required.

To prepare the sauce, remove zest from oranges and lemon, then squeeze out juice. Place butter and sugar cubes in frying pan and leave aside until ready for heating.

To make "Suzette", slowly melt butter and sugar, taking care the butter doesn't brown. When the sugar cubes start to soften, bang them flat with the back of a wooden spoon to speed up melting process! When butter and sugar have melted down (about 2 – 3 minutes) pour in juices and zest, mix well. Fold crêpes in half, then half again and place in frying pan with juices. Bring to the boil slowly, gently heat the crêpes for 2 – 3 minutes, then serve on dessert plates. I like to serve them with a ball of ice cream – Wonderful!

Useful hints:-

If you would like to flambé the crêpes, pour the liqueur into a small saucepan and heat for 2 – 3 minutes. Light with a flame - but take care! Pour lighted liqueur over all the crêpes in the frying pan before serving, or over the individual plates. If you've flambéed before, with confidence, then pour the liqueur straight into the frying pan, heat and ignite.

If you are in Scotland why not call the dish Prince Charlie's Pancakes!

March Menu

Garlic and Parsley Baked Mushrooms

Chicken Fillets with Apricots and Green Peppercorns

Roasted Fan Potatoes

Mange Tout

Small Baby Sweetcorn

Pot au Chocolat

Garlic and Parsley Baked Mushrooms

I love this dish and make it regularly at home for the family as well as a dish suitable for entertaining. You can bake the mushrooms in one large dish then serve them spooned out onto individual dishes, or if you have individual earthenware or gratin dishes then you can bake one large mushroom per person. With this recipe you can make for one person or twenty one!

Ingredients:-
(Serves 4)

4 large flat mushrooms (or 8 smaller ones as they do shrink in cooking).

2 cloves garlic

2 ozs butter

4 – 8 tablespoons double cream (approximately 5 fl. ozs)

2 tablespoons chopped parsley

Method:-

Wipe the mushrooms with a kitchen paper towel to remove dirt, then thickly slice and place either into individual dishes or one large shallow ovenproof dish. Melt butter in saucepan and gently sauté crushed garlic. Spoon those over the mushrooms. To the same pan add the cream, which will mix with the residue butter and garlic and spoon this over mushrooms. Sprinkle with lots of chopped parsley, salt and freshly ground pepper. Leave until ready to cook. Bake in the oven for approximately 15 minutes at 180°C, until cooked. To serve, sprinkle more chopped parsley on the mushrooms and serve with it hot crusty bread, ready to soak up the sauce – delicious!

Useful hints:-

As before, cultivated mushrooms are usually clean, so there is no need to wash or peel them, simply wipe off excess dirt with kitchen paper towel.

Chicken Fillets with Apricots and Green Peppercorns

This chicken dish is interesting with the fruity flavour of apricots and the piquant flavour from the green peppercorns. Green peppercorns in brine can be bought readily from a good delicatessen counter. Any sauce left over (if you were using only 3 - 4 fillets) can be frozen and reused with cooked chicken fillets for a quick supper.

Ingredients:-
(Serves 6)

6 chicken fillets

2 oz butter

1 onion finely chopped

8 oz packet dried apricots

3/4 pint chicken stock
(1 cube to 3/4 pint water)

3 teaspoons drained green peppercorns

Method:-

Although dried apricots no longer require soaking, I soak the apricots in a bowl with boiling water for 10 minutes to soften a little. Drain and roughly puree in food mixer or chop with a knife into small pieces. While allowing the apricots to soak, melt a little butter and quickly seal the chicken fillets on both sides. Place in a shallow ovenproof dish. Melt the remaining butter and sauté the onions until soft but not brown. Add the puree or chopped apricots, green peppercorns and enough stock to make a thick sauce consistency. Pour and spread over the chicken. Season with freshly ground black pepper and cover with tin foil. Leave until ready to cook. Cook at 190°C allowing 35 - 45 minutes depending on size of fillets. After 25 minutes test chicken with skewer, if ready, serve, if not cook for a further 10 - 15 minutes. Sprinkle with chopped parsley or use bunches of watercress to garnish before serving.

Roasted Fan Potatoes / Mange Tout / Baby Sweetcorn

These are baked potatoes with a slant! Just as easy to prepare but looks more interesting for entertaining.

Ingredients: -

1 large potato per person (extra if you wish)

Cooking oil or olive oil

Sea Salt

Method: -

Brush, wash and dry the potatoes. Holding potato firmly, cut 4 - 6 thick slices but only 3/4 way through. Press open a little and place on roasting tray. Brush with oil and sprinkle with sea salt. Bake in oven for approximately 1 hour at 190°C. (put potatoes in oven at the same time as chicken).

Mange Tout
(Serves 6)

8 - 12 ozs mange tout

Mange tout discolours if overcooked or left to keep hot, so cook in boiling salted water or microwave for 3 minutes, just before serving. When cooked, drain well, add a knob of butter and toss well. Serve immediately.

Small
baby sweetcorn
(Serves 6)

8 - 12 ozs baby cobs

Blanch, drain and have ready to cook 5 minutes before serving, or as per instructions. Drain and toss with a knob of butter and sprinkle with black pepper and chopped parsley.

Pot au Chocolat

If you like chocolate, this easy dessert is always a winner. This quantity will give you enough for 4 large ramekin dishes or 4 - 5 small ones. It also looks good in glass or crystal glasses. Serve the dish on a plate or saucer with a paper d'oyly on it. Paper d'oylie's can be bought from kitchen shops, and I use them to make a dessert look special. This dessert can be made during the day and kept in a cold place until ready to serve.

Ingredients:-

4 oz bar of good quality dark eating chocolate

4 oz packet of marshmallows

1 oz unsalted butter

2 eggs

1 tablespoon hot water

Method: -

Melt chocolate in a bowl, either over a pan of boiling water or microwave until soft and melted. (If you microwave please take care not to over cook or the chocolate is wasted). Add marshmallows and melt into chocolate. Stir well. Add the butter and stir until melted. Add the hot water and mix thoroughly until the mixture is smooth. Cool for 5 - 10 minutes. Separate the eggs, drop the yolk into the chocolate and put the white into a bowl. Mix the yolk in well and repeat with the second egg. Using an electric mixer, whisk the egg whites until stiff. Mix one spoonful of egg white into the chocolate and stir in. Now carefully fold in the rest until the mixture is combined. Pour or spoon into the dishes or glasses. Chill until 20 minutes before eating then bring into a warm atmosphere to enhance the flavour of the chocolate. I decorate with a piped star of fresh cream, grated chocolate, chocolate curls or a strawberry!

Useful hints:-

To make cream stars, whip 5 fl.ozs. double cream until stiff, spoon into a piping bag fitted with a large nozzle and pipe onto the dessert. Another tip is to line a baking tray with greaseproof or wax paper and pipe stars onto it. Place the tray in the freezer until the stars are hard, then lift them off carefully and place in a freezer box for protection. Refreeze quickly and leave until you require to jazz up another dessert with cream stars. (They defrost at room temperature in 10-15 minutes.)

April Menu

Stuffed Apple with Tarragon Cream

Chicken Mandalay

Boiled Rice with Toasted Flaked Almonds

Tiramisu

Stuffed Apple with Tarragon Herb Cream

I first tasted this combination of flavours at John Tovey's restaurant and it will always remain a favourite starter. I have changed the dressing a little just to make it easier.

Ingredients:-
(Serves 4)

2 Granny Smith apples

4 ozs soft cream cheese with garlic and chives or herbs

4 ozs rough meat pâté

5 fl. ozs whipping or double cream

1 teaspoon tarragon vinegar or flavoured with herbs

Method: -

Peel apple, remove core and ends and cut in half round the middle. Divide the pâté onto individual serving plates. Fill the hollow core of apple with the cream cheese, turn over and press down onto pâté so rounded half of apple is showing. Whip cream until it's able to hold its shape but not stiff. Gently mix in vinegar at the last moment and immediately spoon over apple to cover completely if possible. Sprinkle a little cayenne or paprika pepper on top for colour. Garnish well with a little salad tossed in vinaigrette dressing or with tarragon, black olives or parsley.

Useful hints:-

This recipe can't be prepared too far in advance as the apple will turn brown, although you can brush with lemon juice. Just have all the ingredients ready in the fridge and the serving plates ready with a suitable garnish.

Substitute pâté for mashed banana, a little chopped dates and nuts for vegetarian guests.

Chicken Mandalay

This is a great recipe for a party or gathering, as the quantity can be increased with no effort. Can be made the day before or frozen, then simply reheated when it is required.

Ingredients:-
(Serves 6)

3 lb chicken (approximately) cooked and cooled, then flesh removed from the bones.

2 ozs margarine

8 ozs onions, peeled and sliced (not chopped)

1 dessertspoons turmeric

2 dessertspoons curry powder (medium strength)

2 dessertspoons plain flour

1/4 teaspoon ground ginger

1 level teaspoon salt

14 oz can tomatoes

1/2 pint chicken stock

2 dessertspoons apricot jam or mango chutney

2 dessertspoons lemon juice

Method: -

In a large pan, melt margarine and sauté onion slices until soft but not brown. Add all ingredients, except chicken, mix well, and allow to simmer for 30 minutes with lid on pan. Check occasionally and stir. Add pieces of chicken, return to simmer point and continue to simmer for 10 minutes. Serve with a sprinkling of chopped parsley.

Useful hints:-

Remember if it's a buffet style dinner, cut the chicken into bite size pieces, if it's a table sitting keep the pieces larger. For this type of recipe I do prefer to boil the chicken rather than roast. Boil in plenty of water for 1 - 2 hours, cool, then remove meat. Do take care to remove the 2 needle like thigh bones as they are often neglected!

Boiled Rice

Boiling rice can give people indigestion! There are so many types of rice and so many methods of cooking rice, it's no wonder there are problems. If you have a good way and successful way stick to it, (no pun intended!!) however, if cooking rice fills you with dread, I will give you a foolproof method.

Ingredients:-
(Serves 4)

1 large pan

2 pints of boiling salted water

2 teacups of long grain rice (Supermarket variety or Basmati)

Method: -

Pour rice straight into boiling water, stir well and let the rice bubble boil for 10 minutes (without lid). Drain into sieve then pour boiling water over the rice in sieve to rinse well. Shake well then tip back into pan. Add approximately 2 ozs toasted flaked almonds and lots of fresh chopped parsley.

Rice can be prepared earlier in the day. Simply follow the above instructions to the point where it is cooked and drained well. Place rice in a shallow ovenproof dish, cover with tinfoil and leave in a cold place. Reheat in a medium oven 180°C for 20 – 30 minutes. Remove foil, fork up and add almonds and parsley.

Useful hints:-

1 teacup or American measuring cup of raw rice serves 2 people. Using a large pan of boiling water gives the rice more room to move around so it doesn't stick. Don't keep rice reheating more than necessary and don't reheat and eat this rice again.

Tiramisu

After spending a holiday with my daughter in Tuscany we became hooked on Tiramisu. This recipe was given to me by a good friend and is quite simply the best I've tasted - delicious!

Ingredients:-
(Serves 6)

1, 125g packet Boudoir sponge fingers

4 fl. ozs strong black coffee or 1/2 teaspoon instant in 4 fl. ozs boiling water

3 tablespoons brandy or any coffee liqueur

3 ozs good quality dark eating chocolate (grated or finely chopped)

3 eggs

4 tablespoons castor sugar

9 oz carton Mascarpone cheese

Cocoa powder (a little)

Method:-

Take three bowls first! In one, mix the cold coffee and liqueur. Separate the eggs, yolks in second bowl, whites in third. Add castor sugar to the yolks and beat until pale and creamy. Fold in the cheese and gently mix well. Whisk the egg whites until stiff and fold into the cheese mixture. Now, with a suitable serving dish ready, dip the sponge fingers individually into the coffee liquid and place a layer in dish. Spoon half the cheese mixture onto sponge fingers, spread well and cover with the chocolate. Repeat a layer of sponge fingers and cheese mixture. Leave to rest for at least 6 hours or overnight. Dust with cocoa powder before serving.

Useful hints:-

Either use a shallow dish, similair to a lasagne type or a glass or crystal dish which allows you to see the layers. As you get approximately 24 sponge fingers in the packet make sure you use an equal quantity per layer!

May Menu

Salad of Asparagus, Avocado and Pine nuts with a Blue Cheese Dressing

Vonda's Chicken

Sesame Rice

Prune Cream

Salad of Asparagus, Avocado and Pine Nuts with a Blue Cheese Dressing

A few years ago I was served something similar to this in a little French restaurant and I thought it was a wonderful salad starter.

Ingredients:-
(Serves 4)

1 packet mixed salad leaves (your choice) or fresh lettuce leaves torn

1 bunch of Asparagus (blanched if baby ones, cooked if large stalks)

1 soft Avocado (never use a hard one – just omit if no soft ones available)

2 ozs toasted pine nuts (sometimes called kernals) – (I toast the whole packet under the grill, cool them, store in a jar, then use for everyday use in salads).

2 ozs fresh parmesan cheese

Dressing

4 ozs soft blue cheese (e.g. Cambozola, Dolcelatte) at room temperature

5 fl. ozs plain yogurt herb vinegar (a little)

Method:-

Remove the hard edges from cheese and cream in a bowl until soft. Add yogurt gradually and beat well. Add enough vinegar to make into a creamy dressing consistency. Keep cool until ready to serve. Using large plain dinner plates, pile some lettuce onto the middle of each plate. Divide asparagus between the plates and place on top of lettuce. Peel and slice avocado and arrange around asparagus. Sprinkle over toasted nuts. Just before serving, drizzle over dressing and using a potato peeler, peel shavings of Parmesan cheese and scatter over salad.

Useful hints:-

If you want to prepare everything before guests arrive, arrange lettuce and asparagus on plates, keep in a cool place, then just before serving, peel and cut the avocado, arrange with nuts, dressing and cheese on plate.

Vonda's Chicken

A good friend served me this wonderful chicken dish 20 years ago. She called it a weird name so I called it "Dorothy's Chicken", you can call it "à la Vonda"!

It has been passed to friends all over the world and it is so easy, (even my husband managed to make it when we had guests staying and I was called away). It's one of those dishes you can make without thinking about it, and can be ready or on standby if you don't know when your guests are arriving. I try to have a cooked chicken (off the bone) in the freezer at all times for such occasions, then when it's defrosted, pour over the sauce and cook it in the oven and it really is fool proof! Ideal for a buffet too!

Ingredients:-
(Serves 4 – 6)

1 cooked chicken (boiled preferably) 3 - 4 lbs

1, 350g jar mango chutney

1 tablespoon medium curry powder (it looks a lot)

10 fl. ozs. plain yoghurt

4 dollops mayonnaise ("dollops" are my measurement for the spoon that fits the jar!)

5 fl. oz carton whipping or double cream

2 ozs toasted flaked almonds

Method:-

Remove all flesh from the chicken and cut into pieces (bite size for buffet, larger for table) and place in a deep ovenproof dish or casserole dish (no lid required). In a saucepan, empty out chutney, cutting the mango slices smaller if you wish. Add curry powder, bring to the boil and simmer gently for 2 minutes. Cool, add mayonnaise and yogurt and stir well. Pour 2/3 over chicken. Leave at this stage until ready to cook in oven. Cook at 190°C for 1 hour. Before serving, pour cream into remaining 1/3 cold sauce left in saucepan, mix well and pour over top of hot chicken. This cold topping covers the top of chicken and makes it look more attractive. Sprinkle with toasted flaked almonds.

Useful hints:-

As before, for chicken dishes like "Mandalay" or "Vonda's" I like to boil the chicken for 1 - 2 hours, this makes them soft and juicy plus you get wonderful stock to freeze.

Sesame Rice

I love using sesame oil as it has such a wonderful rich aroma. Adding it to plain boiled rice is just one of its many uses.

Ingredients:-
(Serves 4)

2 teacups or American cups of long grain rice

2 pints boiling salted water

Sesame oil

1 oz toasted flaked almonds

Freshly chopped parsley

Method:-

Boil the rice for 10 minutes, drain, rinse with boiling water then drain thoroughly again. (See April menu for more details). Return to saucepan. Shake 6 – 8 drops of sesame oil over the rice, and mix well. Spoon out on to hot serving plates or onto a hot serving dish and sprinkle over nuts and lots of chopped parsley.

As before to keep rice hot, cover the dish with tin foil, when ready to serve, fork up, sprinkle over nuts and parsley.

Useful hints:-

Keeping rice warm for hours at a time can lead to food poisoning, so decide for how long you want rice hot. Boil quantities of rice for parties and buffets beforehand and chill. Reheat when you require it throughout the evening. To boil and keep warm for 15 – 30 minutes, no problem! Don't keep and eat re-heated rice.

Prune Cream

I recently met a lady who recognised me as 'the lady who did the Cookery Demonstration at her W.R.I. meeting over 8 years ago', it was lovely to hear her say "I still do your prune dish". What more can I say!

Ingredients:-
(Serves 4)

5 fl. ozs. double cream

5 fl. ozs. plain yogurt

1 small tin prunes (or 4 ozs dried prunes, cooked and cold)

2 tablespoons dark brown sugar (Muscovado)

Method:-

Pour off syrup and de-stone prunes. Whip double cream until stiff and fold in the yogurt carefully. Add the prune bits and mix through. Pour into a pretty serving dish. Sprinkle over the muscovado sugar and allow to sit for a minimum of 20 – 30 minutes as the sugar dissolves and runs over the cream. Keep cool until ready to serve. (This dish will keep, so it can be made hours before).

Useful hints:-

If you don't like the idea of prunes, please try it first, as it is quite delicious. However, if you really don't like prunes then use bananas or raspberries instead. If using an alternative fruit to prunes, use the same fruit flavour of yogurt. This is an excellent dessert for large gatherings of friends!

June Menu

Sole with Orange Mayonnaise

Beef and Wild Mushroom Stroganoff

Flavoured Rice

Profiteroles with Chocolate Sauce

Sole with Orange Mayonnaise

Cold poached sole coated with a light orange flavoured mayonnaise makes a simple starter. However, extend it with an orange salad and crusty bread and you have a wonderful summers day meal which can be prepared before guests arrive.

Ingredients:-
(Serves 6)

6 fillets of fish without skin (ask your fishmonger to skin fillets for you – do not attempt to do it at home without using a good filleting knife!)

Juice of 1/2 lemon

2 oranges (1 orange for zest and juice, and 1 for garnish)

seasoning

1 oz butter

4 dollops mayonnaise

Paprika pepper

Small tin anchovy fillets (optional)

6 wooden cocktail sticks (just checking!)

Method:-

Wash, dry and trim the fillets, then place them all on a board or tray with the removed skin side uppermost. Sprinkle with lemon juice and half the orange juice. Season with a little salt and freshly ground pepper. Sprinkle over orange zest. Roll up fish from head to tail and secure with a cocktail stick. (If you find out now that you have no wooden cocktail sticks you are left holding the fish – literally!) Place the rolled fillets in a shallow buttered ovenproof dish. Pour the remainder of the orange juice over the fish and dot with pieces of butter. Cover with buttered greaseproof or wax paper or tin foil. Bake for 15 – 20 minutes at 180°C until the fillets are tender but still firm. Cool until ready to serve. The fillets can be kept covered until you require them, but remove the cocktail sticks before the fish gets cold. To make the orange mayonnaise, cut the orange in half, squeeze out juice and slowly add to the mayonnaise, otherwise it could curdle. Keep cool until ready to use.

To serve, place the rolled up fillet on a serving plate. Coat with the orange mayonnaise, sprinkle with paprika and arrange two halved anchovies over each fillet. Garnish with a little lettuce or watercress and a slice of the remaining orange (removing the rind and pith first).

Useful hints:-

We are so fortunate to have such fresh fish available here in Scotland, however if Lemon sole is unavailable use Dover sole, Dab or Plaice.

Instructions for filleting fish in the next book, Garith!

Beef and Wild Mushroom Stroganoff

This recipe takes very little time to prepare and cook. Everything can be prepared beforehand and can be cooked 15 minutes before you wish to eat. Double all ingredients if you are serving 6 - 8 people.

Ingredients:-
(Serves 4)

1 lb topside or rump steak

1 onion (chopped)

4 ozs. oyster or wild mushrooms (roughly cut)

2 ozs. butter

1 teaspoon plain flour

1 teaspoon tomato puree

1/2 teaspoon salt

black pepper

1/4 - 1/2 pint chicken (use 1/2 stock cube)

5 fl. ozs. sour cream

chopped parsley

Method:-

Melt 11/2 ozs butter in a saucepan, add mushrooms, sauté, then add onions, cooking until tender. Season, remove from pan and leave aside. Remove all fat from steak and cut into equal manageable pieces, which you now flatten between clingfilm. (A great way to release tension, but be careful you don't thump too hard and tear the meat!). It should be wafer thin. Cut in long finger width strips and place on plate. Season with black pepper. Cover with clingfilm and keep cold until ready to cook.

To cook, melt remaining butter in saucepan, brown beef (in small batches). Sprinkle over flour to absorb juices, and stir well, add tomato puree, stir in, then gradually add enough stock to make a sauce consistency. Add the cooked mushrooms and onions, seal with lid and simmer for 10 minutes checking and adding more stock if required. Just before serving, check seasoning, add sour cream, mix well, and serve with a garnish of chopped parsley.

Boiled Rice

Plain boiled rice is all you need to have with a Stroganoff. However, if you need a change, colour and flavour with saffron or turmeric. Cook the rice while allowing the Stroganoff to simmer.

Ingredients:-
(Serves 4)

2 teacups long grain rice

salt

2 teaspoons turmeric (or pinch saffron threads)

chopped parsley

Method:-

Boil for 10 minutes in boiling salted water, with added turmeric or saffron. Drain and rinse with boiling water, drain again, and return to the saucepan. Add lots of chopped parsley, mix well, and serve immediately.

Useful hints:

A tossed green salad is optional.

Profiteroles with Chocolate sauce

Choux pastry is not a "roll out" pastry but more of a boiled dough, so it really is easy to make and prepare beforehand. When I see the cost of profiteroles in the shops and restaurants I get angry because they are so easy and cheap to make. Please have a try and if you're nervous make them for the family one day then when it comes to entertaining they will be so easy to rustle up!

Ingredients:-

Dough:

3 oz. plain flour

pinch salt

1/4 pint milk & water mixed (I prefer this to all milk)

2 ozs margarine

2 eggs

Sauce:

4 ozs good quality dark eating chocolate

1 small tin evaporated milk

Filling:

1/2 pint whipping or double cream

1 oz icing sugar to sweeten (optional)

Method:-

Place milky water and margarine in a non-stick saucepan and bring to the boil slowly, making sure all the margarine has melted. Immediately remove from heat and add flour and salt. Beat well with a wooden spoon and cook over the heat again for a few seconds until it begins to form a ball and appears glossy. Remove from heat, break up the dough a little, to allow it to cool down quickly, and let it sit for 10 minutes at least. Beat the 2 eggs together, then gradually add a little at a time to the dough and beat well. You must do it gradually as the dough has to absorb the egg in small quantities, otherwise it is almost impossible to mix. (I know, I've been there!) When the dough has absorbed the eggs, beat well and now the dough is ready to use. Grease 2 – 3 baking sheets. This is where you decide how to use the dough. For profiteroles, pipe the dough out into small balls onto the trays. You will get approximately 20 – 25 if you make them the size of a walnut in its shell) and immediately bake in a hot oven. 210°C for 10 minutes, (This allows the air to expand the dough and puff up – do not open the oven door during baking or they will collapse). Turn down the temperature to 160°C and bake for a further 10 minutes, then open door to check they are firm to touch and golden brown. Carefully remove from trays and allow to cool. Whip cream and fill profiteroles – to fill, cut and spoon in cream, or if you have a piping bag, make a hole in profiterole with end of teaspoon or clean pinky finger, then pipe in the cream.

To make the sauce melt chocolate and gradually add enough evaporated milk to make a runny sauce. Pile the profeteroles on to an attractive dish in a pyramid shape, then drizzle over a generous amount of chocolate sauce. Keep cool and before serving, dust with icing sugar. Reheat the remainder of sauce and serve separately.

Useful hints:-

For eclairs, using a plain nozzle pipe 3 – 4 inch fingers, for choux buns, using a dessertspoon, spoon out mixture on to a tray. If you do not have a piping bag and plain nozzle, simply spoon out the dough using a heaped teaspoonful.

July menu

Fresh Asparagus with Hollandaise Sauce

Vonda's Rolled Sole with Smoked Salmon with a Light Leek Sauce

New Baby Potatoes

Courgettes and Green Beans

Pavlova with Fresh Raspberries

Fresh Asparagus with Hollandaise Sauce

I love fresh asparagus! You can use it in many ways, but with melted butter or Hollandaise as an accompaniment - it's perfect! Hollandaise is not complicated, this is an easy method!

Ingredients:-
(Serves 4)

2 bundles of fresh asparagus (at least 6 stalks per person)

Hollandaise Sauce

3 tablespoons wine vinegar

6 peppercorns

1 bay leaf

1 mace blade (or pinch of ground)

2 egg yolks (keep the whites for pavlova!)

seasoning

4 ozs unsalted butter (melted)

Method:-

Place vinegar with spices in a small saucepan and simmer until reduced to approximately 2 teaspoons. Strain into a bowl or electric blender. Add the egg yolks slowly and mix for a second. Beating by hand or in the blender at minimum speed, slowly pour in the melted butter. Sauce made – simple! Make earlier and reheat if you wish.

To serve, cook asparagus as directed, depending on size and amount. (Microwave cooking is excellent for asparagus). At the same time make the sauce or reheat by placing the bowl over a saucepan of simmering water. Arrange the cooked asparagus on individual large hot dinner plates and spoon warm Hollandaise sauce over stems.

Rolled Sole with Smoked Salmon and Light Green Sauce

When I first saw this dish I though it looked good enough to eat! Perfect for summer entertaining.

You will need enough fish for 2 - 3 rolls per person if using it as a main course (a single roll if serving it as a starter). Remember fish cannot wait, so cook only when you are ready to eat. Pop the fish in the oven when you serve the asparagus. The fish sauce is made beforehand, so just re-heat when ready to serve.

Ingredients:-
(Serves 4)

Sauce

8 ozs (approximately 1 large leek) washed

1 oz butter

small bunch watercress (washed)

4 tablespoons dry vermouth or dry sherry

5 fl. oz. single cream

5 fl. oz. fish stock (reserved from cooked sole)

seasoning

Fish

8 sole fillets, without skin and of equal size

4 ozs smoked salmon slices

1 lemon

4 fl. oz. dry white wine

black pepper

8 wooden cocktail sticks

Method:-

Roughly chop leek and sauté in butter. Cover and cook for 5 minutes. Tear up watercress, add to leeks and cook for a further 3 - 4 minutes. Cool and puree with liqueur in a liquidizer or blender. Spoon out into small saucepan and leave until ready to serve with fish.

Wash and dry sole fillets, then place them on a board with the removed skin side uppermost. Arrange slices of smoked salmon on top of each sole fillet, squeeze over with lemon juice and freshly ground black pepper. Roll up from head to tail and secure with wooden cocktail stick. Place in a shallow ovenproof dish, pour over wine, cover with tin foil and leave refrigerated until ready to cook in the oven. (Alternatively, you could poach the sole in a shallow saucepan with lid). When required, cook in the oven for 10 - 15 minutes at 170°C. Remove from oven and carefully spoon out the fish stock and keep fish warm until you finish the sauce. To serve, slowly add cream to leek and watercress puree in saucepan. Heat through but do not allow to boil. Add enough fish stock to make it a sauce consistency. (Add more fish stock rather than cream if preferred). Lift the fish roles on to individual hot dinner plates, remove the cocktail sticks carefully, spoon hot sauce around and over fish roles. Garnish with watercress and lemon slices.

Useful hints:-

As the Rolled Sole with Smoked Salmon is light, fresh and simple, I would suggest plain simple vegetables to accompany.

New Baby Potatoes / Green Beans / Grated Courgettes

Baby potatoes can be bought all year, but to taste the first harvest always reminds me of the days when my Dad would dig up the first potato shaws in the garden and we would gather them up and cook for dinner. They taste so good!!

Ingredients:-
(Serves 4)

Method:-

New Baby Potatoes

1 – 2 lb new baby potatoes (allow 5 – 6 per person)

1 oz butter

1 tablespoon fresh chopped parsley

Brush only to clean the potatoes and boil in salted water for 10 – 15 minutes until cooked. Drain, add butter and parsley, toss and serve.

Green Beans
8 ozs green beans

1 oz butter

Top and tail beans, blanch and drain well. Reserve until ready for cooking. Boil in salted water for 5 – 8 minutes, drain and add freshly ground black pepper.

Grated Courgettes
2 – 3 courgettes

1 oz butter

squeeze of fresh lemon

Wash and dry courgettes, then grate with rough edge grater. Place in saucepan or suitable dish for microwave. Add butter and lemon juice, cover and cook for 2 – 3 minutes. (As courgettes discolour quickly in cooking, cook just before serving).

Pavlova with Fresh Raspberries

Pavlovas come in all shapes and sizes, and a variety of different textures. However, a traditional pavlova should be crispy on the outside with a soft marshmallow texture in the inside. Filled with cream and raspberries, it is a truly mouthwatering dessert! I always make my pavlova on the day of eating, but I know it can be frozen or dried out sufficiently to keep for a few days beforehand. I find it takes minutes to prepare, so I bake it early afternoon so it's still crispy for the evening. I fill it with cream and fruit just before my guests arrive.

Ingredients:-
(Serves 4)

2 egg whites (leftover from Hollandaise sauce!!)

4 ozs castor sugar

1/2 teaspoon vanilla essence

1/2 teaspoon vinegar (any type)

1 teaspoon cornflour

5 – 10 fl ozs whipping cream

8 ozs fresh (or defrosted) raspberries

greaseproof paper or baking parchment

Method:-

Line a baking tray with paper and brush with a little oil. Whisk egg whites until stiff, then add 2 ozs castor sugar, vanilla essence, vinegar and cornflour. Re-whisk until stiff and now shiny in appearance. Fold in remainder of sugar carefully and spoon out on to the middle of tray. Using a knife, spread out meringue to the shape you require. Hollow the centre bringing the mixture up the sides to form a basket. Leave a good 1 inch of space between the pavlova and edges of tray as it expands. Bake in oven for 30 minutes at a moderate heat of 170°C then turn down the temperature to 150°C for 30 – 40 minutes depending on size. This crispens and browns the outside then slowly cooks the inside. When baked, remove from oven, leave to cool for 10 minutes, then, carefully lift and peel off the paper. Place on wire cooling tray, and leave in a dry cool place until evening. Have whipping cream whisked and ready to use (sweetened with icing sugar if desired) and raspberries sprinkled with a little castor sugar if desired, then before guests arrive, place pavlova on serving dish, fill with whipped cream and sprinkle over raspberries. Keep cool until ready to serve at the table.

Useful hints:-

Two egg whites will make a small pavlova, enough for four people, double this recipe and it will make a large one. A round pavlova is the norm but if you don't have a round baking tray or a round serving dish make it rectangle to fit a baking tray and serve on a flat tray.

August menu

Spicy Prawns

Vonda's Cold Chicken with Almonds and Grapes

Sesame Rice

Mixed Leaf Salad with Orange and Strawberries

Drambuie Dreams

Spicy Prawns

This complete menu comprises of cold dishes! It has been a beautiful summer's day and the thought of cooking hot dishes is exhausting! It's relaxing not to cook sometimes, so enjoy this selection of cold foods, all simple to prepare beforehand.

Ingredients:-
(Serves 4)

12 ozs large or tiger cooked peeled prawns

4 cooked prawns in shells (as garnish)

Marinade

3 tablespoons lemon juice

3 spring onions

1 teaspoon finely chopped fresh root ginger

1 teaspoon fresh chopped lemon grass

1 tablespoon fresh chopped mint

Method:-

Put everything (except prawns for garnish) in large bowl and toss well. Cover with cling film and leave in a cool place until ready to serve allowing 30 minutes at least. (If chilling in refrigerator, bring into room temperature 10 – 20 minutes before serving to allow flavours to enhance.

To serve, toss a little green leaf salad selection in lemon juice, pile a little mound on individual plates, spoon prawns and marinade alongside, garnish with a shell prawn, lemon and mint leaf.

Vonda's Cold Chicken with Almonds and Grapes

This recipe calls for a roasted chicken which you can do very easily. However, buying a pre-cooked chicken makes this dish even simpler! One more tip, if you have time to peel and pip grapes fine, if not, buy small seedless grapes and half.

Ingredients:-
(Serves 4)

3 - 4 lb chicken

2 ozs butter

1 wine glass of white dry wine

4 ozs split almonds

2 tablespoon olive oil

8 ozs green grapes (peeled and pipped)

a little lemon juice
seasoning

Dressing

1 wine glass of white dry wine

1/2 lemon juice

1/4 pint olive oil

1 teaspoon chopped herbs
(parsley, mint, chives)

Method:-

Roast chicken with butter and wine in a moderate oven for approximately 2 hours until cooked . Allow to cool and remove all meat. Reserve any juices. (If buying cooked chicken, remove meat in same way). Cut into chunks and place in large bowl. Cover with cling film and keep chilled until ready to serve. Quickly fry almonds in olive oil until golden brown, drain, salt and reserve. Prepare grapes and sprinkle with lemon juice.

Make dressing by boiling wine until it is reduced by half. Cool, add all other ingredients, season and add any chicken juices if you wish.

To serve, bring out bowl of chicken and allow to stand at room temperature for 30 minutes at least, add grapes and dressing, toss well and dish out onto serving plate. Scatter over fried almonds. Garnish with chopped parsley..

Useful hints:-

Instead of opening a good bottle of wine buy a small one. If you need no excuses, open the good bottle, use 2 glasses for recipe and drink the rest!!

Cold Sesame Rice / Mixed Leaf Salad

You may not think of flavouring cold rice with seseme oil - so do try it.

Using only oranges and strawberries gives this salad a colourful look. I sometimes add slices of avocado.

Ingredients:-
(Serves 4)

Remember:-

1 teacup of long grain rice serves 2 persons

(plus 1 teacup for seconds)

Mixed Leaf Salad with Orange and Strawberries

1 packet mixed green leaf salad

1 large orange

6 – 8 strawberries

Dressing

3 tablespoons olive oil

1 tablespoon herb vinegar

1/2 teaspoon whole grain mustard

1/2 teaspoon honey

Method:-

As before, pour 3 cups of long grain rice in to a large pan of boiling salted water. Bring to the boil and bubble boil (without lid) for 10 minutes exactly! Test by eating a grain to ensure it is cooked. Drain and rinse well with cold water to remove starch. Drain again and place in large bowl. Sprinkle over 6 - 8 drops of sesame oil and chopped parsley. Toss and cover with cling film. Keep chilled until ready to serve. Toss again before serving in dish and if desired scatter with toasted flaked almonds.

Place salad leaves in a shallow serving dish or bowl. Cut off peel and pith from the orange using a sharp knife. (Easy to do if you top and tail the orange first then cut down the sides). Either cut the orange into segments or across into slices then into pieces. Any juice from the orange, pour over the salad. Wipe the strawberries with a piece of kitchen paper towel, husk and half (never wash strawberries!). Scatter the orange pieces and strawberries over the salad leaves and serve with dressing when required.

Place all ingredients in screw top jar and shake until mixed thoroughly. Serve in dish or dressing bottle when required. (I make double quantity as it keeps in the fridge for days).

Drambuie Dream with Fruit

This dessert is a variation of 'Glen Mist', a recipe some of you will know well. Simple to prepare but looks very professional!

Ingredients:-
(Serves 4)

10 fl. ozs double or whipping cream

2 tablespoons "runny" honey

4 tablespoons Drambuie liquer (use a miniature)

Method:-

Whip cream with Drambuie and honey until it holds its shape. (If using electric beaters, whisk on slow speed). At this point either cover the bowl with cling film and leave in a cool place (maximum 1 hour) or spoon into 4 ramekin or small dishes and cover.

When ready to serve, place the small dish in the middle of a large plate, and place pieces of prepared fruit around. Decorate with a sprig of mint and dust the entire plate and fruit with icing sugar for that professional finish!

Suggestions for fruit

Strawberries with husk, cut in half (ends dipped in dark chocolate for added interest!)
Raspberries

Thick slices of peeled mango

Thick slices of peeled banana

Small bundles of green and black grapes

Peach slices

Quarters of peeled kiwi fruit

September menu

Asparagus with Warm Leek and Hazelnut Vinaigrette

Pork Fillet with Prunes

New Baby Potatoes

Julienne of Carrots

Mange Tout

Vonda's Trifle

Asparagus with Warm Leek and Hazelnut Vinaigrette

This is an unusual but interesting mixture of texture and flavours. Easy to prepare in advance.

Ingredients:-
(Serves 4)

1 medium leek

4 fl oz chicken or vegetable stock

2 fl oz dry white wine

1 lb asparagus tips (or 2 packets)

2 teaspoons lemon juice

3 tablespoons hazelnut oil (if not, any suitable oil)

3 tablespoons olive oil

2 tablespoons roughly chopped toasted hazelnuts

seasoning

Method:-

Wash the leek very carefully and pat dry. Cut into approximately 2 inch lengths, then cut into fine strips (Julienne!). Place the leeks, stock and wine in a small saucepan, bring to the boil and simmer for approximately 10 – 15 minutes until leek is tender. Meanwhile steam or microwave the asparagus for 3 – 5 minutes until tender or follow instruction on packet. When the leeks are cooked the cooking liquid should have reduced to 2 tablespoons (approximately) if not, remove leeks and bubble boil liquid down. If there is too little liquid add some water; whisk in the lemon juice and oils, season well, then add leeks. Pile asparagus tips onto large plates, spoon over leeks and dressing, sprinkle with the chopped hazelnuts. Serve at room temperature.

Useful hints:-

To prepare beforehand, cook asparagus and leeks as instructed. Keep in a cool place until ready to serve. Arrange as suggested when you wish to eat.

Pork Fillet with Prunes

As pork fillets can vary in size, cater for 2 - 3 thick slices per person (with a little extra for seconds.)

Ingredients:-
(Serves 4)

12 - 15 thick slices of pork fillet (approximately 3/4 inch)

8 ozs large prunes (approximately 20)

10 fl oz dry white wine

seasoned flour (2 tablespoons of plain flour with 1/4 teaspoon salt and ground pepper mixed through)

2 oz butter

5 fl oz double cream

seasoning

lemon juice (1 - 2 tablespoons)

1 heaped tablespoon red currant jelly

Method:-

Leave the prunes soaking in the wine overnight if possible. Next day place prunes and wine in a saucepan, bring to the boil, simmer for 20 - 30 minutes or until tender. Trim any excess fat and sinew off pork, coat with seasoned flour, shaking off any surplus. Melt half the butter in a heavy based pan and brown the pork 3 - 4 slices at one time, turning once. Remove and brown the remainder in the rest of the butter. Replace all the pork back into the pan, cover with a lid and cook gently for 20 - 30 minutes until tender, being careful it does not stick as there is no liquid at this stage. Test the pork with a skewer to check if it is tender. Add prunes and liquid, increase heat and bubble boil for a few seconds. Remove pork and prunes and keep hot. Allow the juices to reduce a little then add red currant jelly, stir well and boil until it resembles a syrup. Gradually add the cream and stir well. Season with salt, freshly ground black pepper and lemon juice. Pour the sauce over the pork slices and arrange the prunes around. Sprinkle with chopped parsley.

Useful hints:-

The dish can be prepared beforehand by browning the pork and leaving it in the pan in a cool place, until ready to cook. Allow approx. 45 minutes cooking time before you wish to eat. Prunes are best soaked overnight.

To accompany the rich, creamy sauce from the pork, plain potatoes and vegetables are all you require.

Ingredients:-
(Serves 4)

New Baby Potatoes

1-2 lb new baby potatoes

1 oz butter

1 tablespoon freshly chopped parsley

Julienne of Carrots

12 ozs carrots

1 oz butter

Mange Tout

8 oz mange tout

1 oz butter

Method:-

Brush potatoes to clean and cook in boiling salted water for approximately 10 minutes until cooked, drain, add butter and parsley, toss well and serve.

Wash and clean carrots, cut into 2 or 3 large pieces then slice lengthwise. Carefully cut into matchstick strips, blanch and drain well. When ready to cook, boil in a little salted water for 5 – 8 minutes, drain, add butter and freshly ground black pepper.

As mange tout discolours very quickly, do not cook and allow to sit. Boil or steam for 2 – 3 minutes, drain and toss in butter and black pepper. Serve immediately.

Vonda's Trifle

This was my Mum's recipe and a favourite for Sunday dinner. Most trifles have a jelly base, this one does not, so the dessert is light and creamy. Easy to make and can be made much earlier in the day. Custard made from powder is quick to make up, however, homemade custard using flour and eggs is equally delicious.

Ingredients:-
(Serves 4 – 6)

1 tin pear halves

1 packet sponge cakes (or homemade sponge cake)

1/2 jar raspberry jam (homemade or good quality jam such as Mackay's of Scotland)

2 sherry glasses of sherry

3/4 pint milk

1 – 2 dessertspoons custard powder

3 – 4 tablespoons granulated sugar

10 fl oz whipping or double cream

4 oz bar good quality dark eating chocolate

Method:-

Using a glass or crystal dish, empty the pears and juice into the bottom. Roughly cut up the pear halves into pieces. Cut the sponge in half and sandwich together with jam. Cut into pieces and place on top of pears. Spread more jam on top and if available, a few thawed frozen raspberries, then drizzle the sherry all over the sponge pieces. Make the custard in the usual way. (Heat milk and sugar in saucepan. Dissolve custard powder in cold milk and slowly add to warm milk. Bring to boil, simmer for a few seconds and allow to cool for a few minutes. Taste and adjust sweetness making it a little sweeter than normal). Pour the custard over the sponge making sure it is completely covered and then smooth the top. Allow to cool completely in a cool area or refrigerator for a few hours. Whip cream until thick then spread on top of custard. Decorate with grated chocolate. Serve at room temperature. (Any leftovers are excellent the following day).

October menu

Tomato, Apple and Celery Soup

Chilli Pork Fillet

Duchess Potatoes

Broccoli Florets

Baby Peas

Oranges in Caramel Sauce

Tomato, Apple and Celery Soup

This soup uses the last of the tomatoes from the greenhouse and windfall apples from the garden. If you, like me, don't grow your own, then buy as usual! However, gifts of greenhouse tomatoes and tasty local Cox's apples make an inexpensive homemade soup. A John Tovey recipe again!

Ingredients:-
(Serves 6 – 8)

2 lb vegetables in total (approx. 10 oz tomatoes, 10 oz apples, 10 oz celery)

2 oz butter

8 oz onions (approx. 2 large)

1/4 pint sherry

salt and freshly ground pepper

2 pints stock, chicken or vegetables

1/4 teaspoon nutmeg (optional)

pinch ground ginger (optional)

Method:-

In a large saucepan, melt the butter and cook the chopped onions until softened. Clean and wash the vegetables, cut the tomatoes in half, leave the skins on the apples and cut into quarters, use the head ends of the celery, including any leaves, which will improve the flavour. (The remainder goes in the pork dish). Add all these to the pan, sprinkle in spices, then add sherry. Cover with a double thickness of wet greaseproof or wax paper. (See January soup for more details). Place on lid and cook gently for 1 hour, shaking often. When cooked add stock, liquidize and sieve. To serve, re-heat to gentle boil, ladle out into warm bowls, and garnish with grated apple or a celery leaf.

Chilli Pork Fillet

This recipe is so simple you almost question "is that all"?

Ingredients:-
(Serves 4)

2 lb pork fillet

4 tablespoons plain flour

2 teaspoons chilli powder

2 cloves garlic (crushed)

1/2 teaspoon salt

1 oz butter

olive oil

2 x 400g tins tomatoes

2 celery stalks

3 oz pine nuts

5 fl oz sour cream

Method:-

Trim fillets of skin and sinew and cut into thick slices (about 1 inch). Mix flour with chilli, crushed garlic and salt, then coat the pork slices. Shake off excess and brown quickly in a frying pan with a little butter and olive oil. Place the pork pieces into a casserole and pour over the tomatoes. Leave in a cool place until ready to cook, for approximately 1 hour at 170°C. Add the finely chopped celery, pine nuts and sour cream, and cook for a further 10 minutes. Serve with a sprinkling of pine nuts.

Useful hints:-

If you feel the sauce is not thick enough, mix a tablespoon of plain flour with 1oz soft butter into a paste, then drop small balls into the sauce while whisking. This will thicken it. (The professional name for this liason is Beurre Manie).

Duchess Potatoes / Broccoli florets / Petit Pois

These potatoes can be prepared beforehand and cooked in the oven along with the casserole. However, if you don't want to make duchess potatoes, follow the recipe but place the creamed potatoes into a buttered shallow dish, dot with knobs of butter and cook as directed.

Ingredients:-
(Serves 4)

1 1/2 - 2 lbs potatoes

salt and pepper

a little milk

1 egg

Method:-

Peel and cut into quarters, boil for 10 – 15 minutes until soft, then drain and mash. Add seasoning, egg and enough milk to make it soft and creamy. When potatoes are cool enough to handle, place in a large piping bag with a large star nozzle. Butter 2 baking trays then pipe out large swirls of potatoes onto trays. Leave in a cool place until ready to cook. Brush with melted butter or leftover egg before browning in the oven. Cook for 15 – 20 minutes in the oven until golden brown.

Broccoli florets

1-1 1/2 lb broccoli

freshly ground black pepper

Remove small florets from stalk and cut into even sizes. Peel thick stalk to reveal soft flesh, then cut into slices. Blanch florets and cut stalk, drain well and leave until ready to cook. Boil in a little salted water for 5-8 minutes until cooked. Drain well and add pepper. Toss and serve.

Baby peas (Petit Pois)

8 ozs peas

1 oz butter

Cook peas in boiling salted water for 2-3 minutes, or as directed on the packet. Drain and serve. (For added interest, sauté a small shallot, finely chopped, then mix with peas, or add lots of fresh, washed, garden mint, or shredded lettuce).

Oranges in Caramel Sauce

Oranges at this time of the year are small and sweet and usually come in bags of 10. Great way to use up these oranges!

Ingredients:-
(Serves 4)

6 small oranges

6 oz soft brown sugar

6 oz water

2 tablespoons brandy or orange liqueur

Method:-

Using a sharp knife top, tail and cut off orange skin ,(including the white pith) and cut into slices, reserving all the juices while you're slicing. Put slices and juice into a glass or crystal serving dish or shallow dish. Put water and sugar into a saucepan and bring to the boil, stirring frequently. Allow to cool, add liqueur and pour over oranges. Serve at room temperature. The oranges taste delicious on their own but a jug or bowl of creamy yogurt, cream or crème fraiche will go down well!

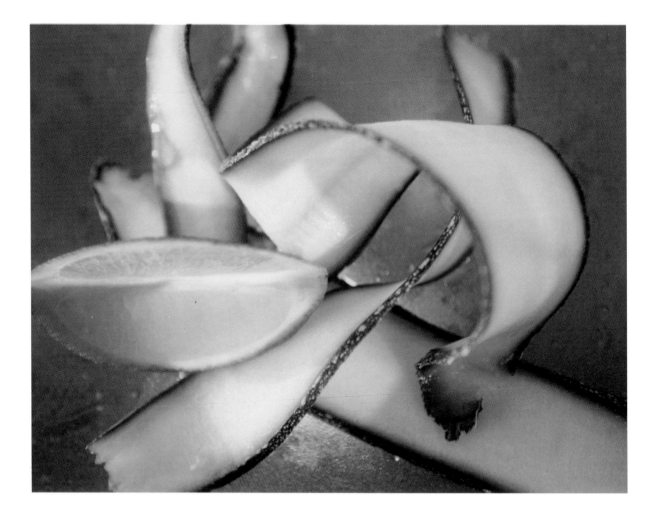

November Menu

Ribbon of Smoked Salmon on a Fan of Avocado with Lime Mayonnaise

Pork Fillet Casserole

Turmeric and Black Peppered Potatoes

Sliced Courgettes

Baby Cobs

Apple Streusel

Ribbons of Smoked Salmon on a Fan of Avocado with Lime Mayonnaise

This is a very attractive and easy starter suitable for serving 2 - 12 people! Use more smoked salmon if you wish.

Ingredients:-
(Serves 4)

4 – 6 oz Scottish smoked salmon slices (pre-sliced in packet)

2 soft avocados

fresh dill

2 limes

3 dessertspoons good mayonnaise

Method:-

Cut the smoked salmon slices into fine shreds (Julienne). Lift and separate the shreds and place a mound on four large serving plates. Peel and halve the avocados, remove stones and either cut into thin slices or fan by cutting into thin slices leaving the top end whole. Lift carefully onto plate and arrange alongside salmon. Remove the zest and juice from one lime and place in a small bowl. Using a pastry brush, brush a little lime juice over the avocado to prevent them discolouring. (Remove the plates of salmon and avocado to a cool place if allowing to stand any longer than 15 minutes). Drop the mayonnaise into the remainder of lime juice and zest, whisk through until it is creamy and smooth.

To serve, spoon the lime mayonnaise around the avocado and a little over it. Place a sprig of dill on top and with the remaining lime, cut into slices or wedges and place by the salmon.

Pork Fillet Casserole

This is a lovely casserole where everything is prepared beforehand and cooked slowly so you can enjoy a relaxed evening! Double up all the ingredients if you require more.

Ingredients:-
(Serves 4)

1 1/2 - 2 lbs pork fillet

seasoned flour (plain flour with seasoning)

2 oz butter

2 onions

1 large leek

4 oz celery

1 green pepper

1 400g tin tomatoes

1/4 pint tomato juice or cider

1 tablespoon good vinegar (white wine, cider or herb vinegar)

Method:-

Trim fillet, removing skin and sinew, then cut into slices. Dust in seasoned flour and brown quickly in 1 oz of butter in a frying pan. (brown 4 - 5 slices only at one time). Remove from butter and place in a casserole dish or ovenproof dish. Wash, clean and trim all vegetables, chop, and with the remainder of butter, saute for 10 minutes. Add the tomatoes, vinegar, cider or tomato juice. Pour this all over the pork slices, cover with a lid or tin foil and allowing 1 hour for slow cooking, keep in a cool place until ready to cook at 160°C.

To serve, stir well, taste and adjust seasoning, and sprinkle with chopped parsley.

Useful hints:-
Thicken the sauce with a little Beurre Manie if you wish.

74

Turmeric and Black Peppered Potatoes / Courgettes / Baby cobs

As you're not busy preparing the main course these potatoes do need a little preparation at the last minute. The lovely rich colour of turmeric give old potatoes a brand new look!

Ingredients:-
(Serves 4)

2 lb potatoes

oil (approximately 3 – 4 tablespoons)

1 teaspoon turmeric

1/2 teaspoon freshly ground black pepper

Method:-

Peel and cut potatoes into quarters, then boil in salted water until cooked but not too soft. Drain well and leave until ready to serve. To serve, heat oil in a frying pan, taking care, add the turmeric and pepper. Quickly add the potatoes and toss well so all the potatoes are coated in turmeric and pepper. Allow to heat through, tossing often, and when you see them browning a little, remove and drain on a kitchen paper towel. Serve in a hot dish with a sprinkling of chopped parsley.

Courgettes in butter

3 – 4 courgettes

1 oz butter

Cut courgettes in slices and when ready to serve melt butter in a saucepan, add courgettes and toss for 2 – 3 minutes. Alternatively, using a wide vegetable peeler, cut ribbons lengthwise down courgette and cook as directed.

Baby cobs
(allow 4 – 5 per person)

Place in boiling salted water to cook for 3 – 5 minutes. Drain well, add a knob of butter, black pepper, toss well and serve.

Apple Streusel

This is a delicious apple tart with a crunchy hazelnut topping. If pastry making scares you, then buy ready made shortcrust pastry and then follow the method - simple!

Ingredients:-
(Serves 4 – 8)

6 oz short crust pastry

1lb cooking apples

2 oz castor sugar

1 level tablespoon cornflour

1 oz sultanas or raisins

Topping

4 oz plain flour

3 oz margarine

2 oz soft brown sugar

3 tablespoons chopped toasted hazelnuts

Method:-

Roll out the pastry (turning the pastry, not the rolling pin , remember!) and line a fluted flan dish. Peel and slice apples, pile into the case, then sprinkle over the sultanas or raisins. Mix the cornflour and castor sugar together and then sprinkle this over apples. (This absorbs the apple juices and prevents it soaking the pastry). In a large bowl, rub the margarine into flour, add the brown sugar, then 2 tablespoons of hazelnuts. Carefully sprinkle this mixture over the apples and press down well. Sprinkle the remaining hazelnuts on top. Bake at 200°C for 20 minutes then reduce the heat to 180°C and bake for a further 15 – 20 minutes until golden brown. Allow to cool a little before serving with cream. (This tart can be baked in advance and served cold, or reheat for 15-20 minutes in a warm oven before serving).

Useful hints:-

Short crust pastry

4 oz plain flour and 2 oz hard margarine (rubbed together)

1 tablespoon castor sugar dissolved in 1 tablespoon boiling water.

Method:-

Add sugar and water to flour and margarine and mix with enough cold water to make a dough. Keep cool until required.

December menu

Filo Parcels with Brie, Celery and
Walnuts on a Raspberry Couli

Chicken Breasts with Tarragon and
Gruyere Cheese

Duchess Potatoes

Asparagus tips

Mange Tout

Gâteau Paris – Brest

Filo Parcels with Brie, Celery and Walnut on a Raspberry Couli

Working with Filo pastry is not difficult, just needs more time than 5 minutes! The filling is my suggestion, you can use whatever you like and you could use a Cranberry Couli if you prefer.

Ingredients:-
(Serves 4)

1 packet Filo pastry sheets, defrosted

2 – 4 oz butter

4 oz Brie cheese

2 stalks celery

1 oz chopped walnuts or pecan nuts

4 oz raspberries (if frozen, defrosted)

1 tablespoon icing sugar

Method:-

Melt a little of the butter in a saucepan and sauté finely chopped celery until soft, add chopped nuts and season with a little salt and freshly ground black pepper. Allow to cool. Melt the remaining butter. Cut the cheese into 4 pieces and keep cool while working with the pastry. Bring out 2-4 sheets depending on its size and measure up enough pastry to cut 8 squares approximately 4 inch x 4 inch. Brush all the squares with melted butter and place 2 squares on top of each other diagonally. Place the cheese piece in the middle and pile a little celery and walnut on top. Bring up the pastry ends using both your hands to gather together and press into an "old purse" shape. Lift onto greased or non-stick baking trays. Brush with more melted butter and leave in a cool place until ready to bake for 20 minutes at 180°C. Press the raspberries through a fine sieve and collect the juice and puree. Mix in the icing sugar and taste. (Add more sugar if you wish). Keep cool until required. To serve, spoon a tablespoon of raspberry couli onto each of the large serving plates. Carefully lift the baked filo parcels onto the plate and garnish with celery leaves, a few extra chopped nuts or raspberries scattered over the plate.

Useful hints:-

You may not use the whole packet of filo pastry for this recipe, so re-wrap the remainder of sheets again, re-freeze or keep chilled and use within a few days. Couli is the 'in' word to describe a cold fruit sauce.

Chicken Breasts with Tarragon and Gruyere Cheese

This is a very easy chicken dish cooked in a saucepan rather than the oven, but it does mean you do need to be in the kitchen cooking for a little while.

Ingredients:-
(Serves 4)

4 large chicken fillets

salt and freshly ground black pepper

3 oz butter

2 tablespoons plain flour

10 fl oz chicken stock

1 tablespoon chopped fresh tarragon or 1/2 teaspoon dried

5 fl oz sour cream

2 oz Gruyere cheese, grated

1 tablespoon freshly grated Parmesan cheese

Method:-

Wash, trim and dry chicken fillets, then season with salt and black pepper. Melt 2 oz butter in a large shallow saucepan and brown the chicken fillets cooking for 3 – 4 minutes each side, then remove from pan. Melt the remaining butter in the pan, add the flour and mix well, then gradually mix or whisk in the stock. Add the fresh tarragon, bring to the boil, then return the chicken fillets, reduce the heat to a gentle simmer, cover and cook for 20 – 30 minutes until the chicken is cooked. To serve, remove fillets, keep hot, remove saucepan from heat, add cream and cheeses and stir until melted. Do not bring back to the boil as this will toughen the cheese. Adjust seasoning, serve fillets on hot plates, coat with tarragon sauce and garnish with sprigs of fresh tarragon.

Duchess Potatoes / Asparagus Tips

These potatoes will look attractive with the chicken and can be cooked in the oven with the filo parcel. Cook and prepare earlier in the day. Allow 2 - 3 swirls per person.

Ingredients:-
(Serves 4)

2 lb potatoes

1/4 pint milk

1 egg (beaten)

1 oz butter

seasoning

Method:-

As before, cook potatoes until soft, drain well and mash. Add the butter, egg and enough milk to make them soft. Spoon into large piping bag and pipe onto greased baking trays several large swirls about 2 inches wide by 3 - 4 inches high. Leave in a cool place until ready to be baked in the oven. Before baking, dot with a knob of butter or brush with beaten egg. Place in the oven at 180°C for 15 - 20 minutes along with the filo parcels. Remove carefully with a fish slice. Sprinkle with chopped parsley.

Asparagus Tips

2 packets asparagus tips (allowing approximately 4 - 6 tips per person)

Prepare and cook as directed or boil in salted water for 2 - 3 minutes. Drain and toss in a little butter and freshly ground black pepper. Serve mange tout or broccoli florets if you require more vegetables.

Gateau Paris - Brest

This wonderful French gateau originated in the late 19th century in honour of a famous bicycle race from Paris to Brest. Made from choux pastry, it looks impressive, but is very easy to make beforehand. You will need a large piping bag and plain nozzle.

Ingredients:-
(Serves 4 – 8)

1 oz unsalted butter

1 level teaspoon castor sugar

1/4 pint milk

4 oz plain flour

3 eggs

1-2 oz flaked almonds

1/2 pint double cream

3 level tablespoons icing sugar

Method:-

Put the milk, butter and castor sugar in a saucepan (preferably non-stick) and bring to the boil slowly making sure all the butter melts. Take off the heat and add the flour. Mix thoroughly with a wooden spoon until it leaves the sides clean and looks glossy. Allow the dough to cool while you beat 2 eggs in a bowl. Add a little beaten egg to the dough and beat well until it is absorbed. (Never hurry this process and add more – trust me!). When the two eggs are absorbed and you feel it is still too stiff for piping add the third egg. Spoon the dough into the piping bag and pipe a ring about 1 inch wide by 8 inches in diameter onto a greased baking tray. If you don't want to use a piping bag – using a teaspoon, spoon a circle of dough and spread to join up. Sprinkle the almonds over the dough and bake for 30 minutes at 200°C. (Don't open the door before 25 minutes, unless it is in flames!). The pastry should be a dark golden brown colour, well risen and crispy. Cool the pastry ring and then cut in half horizontally with a sharp knife. If there are any areas of uncooked dough, just remove and discard. Whip the double cream with 2 tablespoons of icing sugar until stiff. Spoon the cream into the hollow bottom half, cover with the top, and dust with the remaining sifted icing sugar. Lift onto an attractive flat plate to serve and keep cool, but bring to room temperature before eating.

For something special try a few tablespoons of Drambuie liqueur in the cream! French with a Scottish twist?

Useful hints:-

As a guide for piping or spooning out the choux pastry onto the greased baking tray, take a suitable size plate or pan lid to fit the baking tray, lightly dust with flour, remove the lid or plate and you have a circle!!

Whatever the seasoning,

Whatever the dish,

Whatever the occasion, do it

generously and with love,

for that in the end, is what

the shared experience

of cooking and eating

is all about.

(Elizabeth Rozin)

Index

Index